Smoke Free in 2020

Belongs to

____

____

Congratulations

Welcome and a huge congratulations
on taking the first and

most important step

in your stop smoking resolution.

This book was created to help folks,

just like you, kick the smoking habit.

Getting Ready to Break the Habit

Breaking habits is not an easy thing to do.

Experts state, one can usually break a habit in 21 days. In my opinion, smoking is a much larger beast.

We are going to work through 60 days in this workbook. Perhaps you won't need all 60 or perhaps you'll need a second (or third) workbook.

This is YOUR life and it is special and unique.

We'll be going day by day – for 60 days.

You'll find some affirmations as well as daily logs. The note pages, every 7 days, is for logging your thoughts, feelings and and/or progress, if you so choose.

Ideally, as you progress, you will see some patterns – what makes you want to smoke, what time of day, even certain foods.

Use this information to create new routines and set yourself up to win.

You CAN do this – I have full faith in your success.

Sincerely,
Diana

Affirmations to Help Stop Smoking

Every time I need a break, I just breathe and let go.

I love myself more
than I love smoking.

I say yes to
life and no to
smoking.

Since I know my self better every day, I know how to stop smoking with ease.

When I am feeling stressed, unhappy or sad, I am taking a quick walk and will breathe deeply and calmly.

I feel great as I breathe in the fresh air.

I am free from smoking today and I am very happy about it. I feel so much better.

I breathe so much better and am feeling the improvement every day.

I am free from
smoking today
and I'm so happy
about it.

I breathe so much better and enjoy eating fresh fruits and vegetables.

I care and respect my body and have let go of unhealthy addictions.

I am in control of
my life.

Quit Smoking Tracker   Date

Time	Number of cigarettes GOALS	Total cigarettes smoked
01:00		
02:00		
03:00		
04:00		
05:00		
06:00		
07:00		
08:00		
09:00		
10:00		
11:00		
12:00		
13:00		
14:00		
15:00		
16:00		
17:00		
18:00		
19:00		
20:00		
21:00		
22:00		
23:00		
24:00		

Quit Smoking Tracker   Day 1

Occasion	Mood	Food/Drink	Urgency Level
			Low Med. High
			Low Med. High
			Low Med. High
			Low Med. High
			Low Med. High
			Low Med. High
			Low Med. High
			Low Med. High
			Low Med. High
			Low Med. High
			Low Med. High
			Low Med. High
			Low Med. High
			Low Med. High
			Low Med. High
			Low Med. High
			Low Med. High
			Low Med. High
			Low Med. High
			Low Med. High
			Low Med. High
			Low Med. High
			Low Med. High
			Low Med. High

Quit Smoking Tracker Date

Time	Number of cigarettes GOALS	Total cigarettes smoked

Quit Smoking Tracker   Day 2

Occasion	Mood	Food/Drink	Urgency Level
			Low Med. High
			Low Med. High
			Low Med. High
			Low Med. High
			Low Med. High
			Low Med. High
			Low Med. High
			Low Med. High
			Low Med. High
			Low Med. High
			Low Med. High
			Low Med. High
			Low Med. High
			Low Med. High
			Low Med. High
			Low Med. High
			Low Med. High
			Low Med. High
			Low Med. High
			Low Med. High
			Low Med. High
			Low Med. High
			Low Med. High

Quit Smoking Tracker   Date

Time	Number of cigarettes GOALS	Total cigarettes smoked
01:00		
02:00		
03:00		
04:00		
05:00		
06:00		
07:00		
08:00		
09:00		
10:00		
11:00		
12:00		
13:00		
14:00		
15:00		
16:00		
17:00		
18:00		
19:00		
20:00		
21:00		
22:00		
23:00		
24:00		

Quit Smoking Tracker   Day 3

Occasion	Mood	Food/Drink	Urgency Level
			Low Med. High
			Low Med. High
			Low Med. High
			Low Med. High
			Low Med. High
			Low Med. High
			Low Med. High
			Low Med. High
			Low Med. High
			Low Med. High
			Low Med. High
			Low Med. High
			Low Med. High
			Low Med. High
			Low Med. High
			Low Med. High
			Low Med. High
			Low Med. High
			Low Med. High
			Low Med. High
			Low Med. High
			Low Med. High
			Low Med. High

Quit Smoking Tracker   Date

Time	Number of cigarettes GOALS	Total cigarettes smoked
01:00		
02:00		
03:00		
04:00		
05:00		
06:00		
07:00		
08:00		
09:00		
10:00		
11:00		
12:00		
13:00		
14:00		
15:00		
16:00		
17:00		
18:00		
19:00		
20:00		
21:00		
22:00		
23:00		
24:00		

Quit Smoking Tracker   Day 4

Occasion	Mood	Food/Drink	Urgency Level
			Low Med. High
			Low Med. High
			Low Med. High
			Low Med. High
			Low Med. High
			Low Med. High
			Low Med. High
			Low Med. High
			Low Med. High
			Low Med. High
			Low Med. High
			Low Med. High
			Low Med. High
			Low Med. High
			Low Med. High
			Low Med. High
			Low Med. High
			Low Med. High
			Low Med. High
			Low Med. High
			Low Med. High
			Low Med. High

Quit Smoking Tracker   Date

Time	Number of cigarettes GOALS	Total cigarettes smoked
01:00		
02:00		
03:00		
04:00		
05:00		
06:00		
07:00		
08:00		
09:00		
10:00		
11:00		
12:00		
13:00		
14:00		
15:00		
16:00		
17:00		
18:00		
19:00		
20:00		
21:00		
22:00		
23:00		
24:00		

Quit Smoking Tracker Day 5

Occasion	Mood	Food/Drink	Urgency Level
			Low Med. High
			Low Med. High
			Low Med. High
			Low Med. High
			Low Med. High
			Low Med. High
			Low Med. High
			Low Med. High
			Low Med. High
			Low Med. High
			Low Med. High
			Low Med. High
			Low Med. High
			Low Med. High
			Low Med. High
			Low Med. High
			Low Med. High
			Low Med. High
			Low Med. High
			Low Med. High
			Low Med. High
			Low Med. High

Quit Smoking Tracker   Date

Time	Number of cigarettes GOALS	Total cigarettes smoked
01:00		
02:00		
03:00		
04:00		
05:00		
06:00		
07:00		
08:00		
09:00		
10:00		
11:00		
12:00		
13:00		
14:00		
15:00		
16:00		
17:00		
18:00		
19:00		
20:00		
21:00		
22:00		
23:00		
24:00		

Quit Smoking Tracker   Day 6

Occasion	Mood	Food/Drink	Urgency Level
			Low Med. High
			Low Med. High
			Low Med. High
			Low Med. High
			Low Med. High
			Low Med. High
			Low Med. High
			Low Med. High
			Low Med. High
			Low Med. High
			Low Med. High
			Low Med. High
			Low Med. High
			Low Med. High
			Low Med. High
			Low Med. High
			Low Med. High
			Low Med. High
			Low Med. High
			Low Med. High
			Low Med. High
			Low Med. High
			Low Med. High
			Low Med. High
			Low Med. High

Quit Smoking Tracker   Date

Time	Number of cigarettes GOALS	Total cigarettes smoked
01:00		
02:00		
03:00		
04:00		
05:00		
06:00		
07:00		
08:00		
09:00		
10:00		
11:00		
12:00		
13:00		
14:00		
15:00		
16:00		
17:00		
18:00		
19:00		
20:00		
21:00		
22:00		
23:00		
24:00		

Quit Smoking Tracker   Day 7

Occasion	Mood	Food/Drink	Urgency Level
			Low Med. High
			Low Med. High
			Low Med. High
			Low Med. High
			Low Med. High
			Low Med. High
			Low Med. High
			Low Med. High
			Low Med. High
			Low Med. High
			Low Med. High
			Low Med. High
			Low Med. High
			Low Med. High
			Low Med. High
			Low Med. High
			Low Med. High
			Low Med. High
			Low Med. High
			Low Med. High
			Low Med. High
			Low Med. High

Quit Smoking Tracker

Quit Smoking Tracker

Quit Smoking Tracker   Date

Time	Number of cigarettes GOALS	Total cigarettes smoked
01:00		
02:00		
03:00		
04:00		
05:00		
06:00		
07:00		
08:00		
09:00		
10:00		
11:00		
12:00		
13:00		
14:00		
15:00		
16:00		
17:00		
18:00		
19:00		
20:00		
21:00		
22:00		
23:00		
24:00		

Quit Smoking Tracker   Day 8

Occasion	Mood	Food/Drink	Urgency Level
			Low Med. High
			Low Med. High
			Low Med. High
			Low Med. High
			Low Med. High
			Low Med. High
			Low Med. High
			Low Med. High
			Low Med. High
			Low Med. High
			Low Med. High
			Low Med. High
			Low Med. High
			Low Med. High
			Low Med. High
			Low Med. High
			Low Med. High
			Low Med. High
			Low Med. High
			Low Med. High
			Low Med. High
			Low Med. High

Quit Smoking Tracker   Date

Time	Number of cigarettes GOALS	Total cigarettes smoked
01:00		
02:00		
03:00		
04:00		
05:00		
06:00		
07:00		
08:00		
09:00		
10:00		
11:00		
12:00		
13:00		
14:00		
15:00		
16:00		
17:00		
18:00		
19:00		
20:00		
21:00		
22:00		
23:00		
24:00		

Quit Smoking Tracker   Day 9

Occasion	Mood	Food/Drink	Urgency Level
			Low Med. High
			Low Med. High
			Low Med. High
			Low Med. High
			Low Med. High
			Low Med. High
			Low Med. High
			Low Med. High
			Low Med. High
			Low Med. High
			Low Med. High
			Low Med. High
			Low Med. High
			Low Med. High
			Low Med. High
			Low Med. High
			Low Med. High
			Low Med. High
			Low Med. High
			Low Med. High
			Low Med. High
			Low Med. High
			Low Med. High

Quit Smoking Tracker   Date

Time	Number of cigarettes GOALS	Total cigarettes smoked
01:00		
02:00		
03:00		
04:00		
05:00		
06:00		
07:00		
08:00		
09:00		
10:00		
11:00		
12:00		
13:00		
14:00		
15:00		
16:00		
17:00		
18:00		
19:00		
20:00		
21:00		
22:00		
23:00		
24:00		

Quit Smoking Tracker   Day 10

Occasion	Mood	Food/Drink	Urgency Level
			Low Med. High
			Low Med. High
			Low Med. High
			Low Med. High
			Low Med. High
			Low Med. High
			Low Med. High
			Low Med. High
			Low Med. High
			Low Med. High
			Low Med. High
			Low Med. High
			Low Med. High
			Low Med. High
			Low Med. High
			Low Med. High
			Low Med. High
			Low Med. High
			Low Med. High
			Low Med. High
			Low Med. High
			Low Med. High
			Low Med. High

Quit Smoking Tracker   Date

Time	Number of cigarettes GOALS	Total cigarettes smoked
01:00		
02:00		
03:00		
04:00		
05:00		
06:00		
07:00		
08:00		
09:00		
10:00		
11:00		
12:00		
13:00		
14:00		
15:00		
16:00		
17:00		
18:00		
19:00		
20:00		
21:00		
22:00		
23:00		
24:00		

Quit Smoking Tracker   Day 11

Occasion	Mood	Food/Drink	Urgency Level
			Low Med. High
			Low Med. High
			Low Med. High
			Low Med. High
			Low Med. High
			Low Med. High
			Low Med. High
			Low Med. High
			Low Med. High
			Low Med. High
			Low Med. High
			Low Med. High
			Low Med. High
			Low Med. High
			Low Med. High
			Low Med. High
			Low Med. High
			Low Med. High
			Low Med. High
			Low Med. High
			Low Med. High
			Low Med. High
			Low Med. High

Quit Smoking Tracker   Date

Time	Number of cigarettes GOALS	Total cigarettes smoked
01:00		
02:00		
03:00		
04:00		
05:00		
06:00		
07:00		
08:00		
09:00		
10:00		
11:00		
12:00		
13:00		
14:00		
15:00		
16:00		
17:00		
18:00		
19:00		
20:00		
21:00		
22:00		
23:00		
24:00		

Quit Smoking Tracker   Day 12

Occasion	Mood	Food/Drink	Urgency Level
			Low Med. High
			Low Med. High
			Low Med. High
			Low Med. High
			Low Med. High
			Low Med. High
			Low Med. High
			Low Med. High
			Low Med. High
			Low Med. High
			Low Med. High
			Low Med. High
			Low Med. High
			Low Med. High
			Low Med. High
			Low Med. High
			Low Med. High
			Low Med. High
			Low Med. High
			Low Med. High
			Low Med. High
			Low Med. High
			Low Med. High

Quit Smoking Tracker   Date

Time	Number of cigarettes GOALS	Total cigarettes smoked
01:00		
02:00		
03:00		
04:00		
05:00		
06:00		
07:00		
08:00		
09:00		
10:00		
11:00		
12:00		
13:00		
14:00		
15:00		
16:00		
17:00		
18:00		
19:00		
20:00		
21:00		
22:00		
23:00		
24:00		

Quit Smoking Tracker   Day 13

Occasion	Mood	Food/Drink	Urgency Level
			Low Med. High
			Low Med. High
			Low Med. High
			Low Med. High
			Low Med. High
			Low Med. High
			Low Med. High
			Low Med. High
			Low Med. High
			Low Med. High
			Low Med. High
			Low Med. High
			Low Med. High
			Low Med. High
			Low Med. High
			Low Med. High
			Low Med. High
			Low Med. High
			Low Med. High
			Low Med. High
			Low Med. High
			Low Med. High
			Low Med. High

Quit Smoking Tracker   Date

Time	Number of cigarettes GOALS	Total cigarettes smoked
01:00		
02:00		
03:00		
04:00		
05:00		
06:00		
07:00		
08:00		
09:00		
10:00		
11:00		
12:00		
13:00		
14:00		
15:00		
16:00		
17:00		
18:00		
19:00		
20:00		
21:00		
22:00		
23:00		
24:00		

Quit Smoking Tracker   Day 14

Occasion	Mood	Food/Drink	Urgency Level
			Low Med. High
			Low Med. High
			Low Med. High
			Low Med. High
			Low Med. High
			Low Med. High
			Low Med. High
			Low Med. High
			Low Med. High
			Low Med. High
			Low Med. High
			Low Med. High
			Low Med. High
			Low Med. High
			Low Med. High
			Low Med. High
			Low Med. High
			Low Med. High
			Low Med. High
			Low Med. High
			Low Med. High
			Low Med. High
			Low Med. High

Quit Smoking Tracker

Quit Smoking Tracker

Quit Smoking Tracker   Date

Time	Number of cigarettes GOALS	Total cigarettes smoked
01:00		
02:00		
03:00		
04:00		
05:00		
06:00		
07:00		
08:00		
09:00		
10:00		
11:00		
12:00		
13:00		
14:00		
15:00		
16:00		
17:00		
18:00		
19:00		
20:00		
21:00		
22:00		
23:00		
24:00		

Quit Smoking Tracker   Day 15

Occasion	Mood	Food/Drink	Urgency Level
			Low Med. High
			Low Med. High
			Low Med. High
			Low Med. High
			Low Med. High
			Low Med. High
			Low Med. High
			Low Med. High
			Low Med. High
			Low Med. High
			Low Med. High
			Low Med. High
			Low Med. High
			Low Med. High
			Low Med. High
			Low Med. High
			Low Med. High
			Low Med. High
			Low Med. High
			Low Med. High
			Low Med. High
			Low Med. High

Quit Smoking Tracker   Date

Time	Number of cigarettes GOALS	Total cigarettes smoked
01:00		
02:00		
03:00		
04:00		
05:00		
06:00		
07:00		
08:00		
09:00		
10:00		
11:00		
12:00		
13:00		
14:00		
15:00		
16:00		
17:00		
18:00		
19:00		
20:00		
21:00		
22:00		
23:00		
24:00		

Quit Smoking Tracker   Day 16

Occasion	Mood	Food/Drink	Urgency Level
			Low Med. High
			Low Med. High
			Low Med. High
			Low Med. High
			Low Med. High
			Low Med. High
			Low Med. High
			Low Med. High
			Low Med. High
			Low Med. High
			Low Med. High
			Low Med. High
			Low Med. High
			Low Med. High
			Low Med. High
			Low Med. High
			Low Med. High
			Low Med. High
			Low Med. High
			Low Med. High
			Low Med. High
			Low Med. High

Quit Smoking Tracker Date

Time	Number of cigarettes GOALS	Total cigarettes smoked
01:00		
02:00		
03:00		
04:00		
05:00		
06:00		
07:00		
08:00		
09:00		
10:00		
11:00		
12:00		
13:00		
14:00		
15:00		
16:00		
17:00		
18:00		
19:00		
20:00		
21:00		
22:00		
23:00		
24:00		

Quit Smoking Tracker   Day 17

Occasion	Mood	Food/Drink	Urgency Level
			Low Med. High
			Low Med. High
			Low Med. High
			Low Med. High
			Low Med. High
			Low Med. High
			Low Med. High
			Low Med. High
			Low Med. High
			Low Med. High
			Low Med. High
			Low Med. High
			Low Med. High
			Low Med. High
			Low Med. High
			Low Med. High
			Low Med. High
			Low Med. High
			Low Med. High
			Low Med. High
			Low Med. High
			Low Med. High

Quit Smoking Tracker   Date

Time	Number of cigarettes GOALS	Total cigarettes smoked
01:00		
02:00		
03:00		
04:00		
05:00		
06:00		
07:00		
08:00		
09:00		
10:00		
11:00		
12:00		
13:00		
14:00		
15:00		
16:00		
17:00		
18:00		
19:00		
20:00		
21:00		
22:00		
23:00		
24:00		

Occasion	Mood	Food/Drink	Urgency Level
			Low Med. High
			Low Med. High
			Low Med. High
			Low Med. High
			Low Med. High
			Low Med. High
			Low Med. High
			Low Med. High
			Low Med. High
			Low Med. High
			Low Med. High
			Low Med. High
			Low Med. High
			Low Med. High
			Low Med. High
			Low Med. High
			Low Med. High
			Low Med. High
			Low Med. High
			Low Med. High
			Low Med. High
			Low Med. High

Quit Smoking Tracker   Date

Time	Number of cigarettes GOALS	Total cigarettes smoked
01:00		
02:00		
03:00		
04:00		
05:00		
06:00		
07:00		
08:00		
09:00		
10:00		
11:00		
12:00		
13:00		
14:00		
15:00		
16:00		
17:00		
18:00		
19:00		
20:00		
21:00		
22:00		
23:00		
24:00		

Quit Smoking Tracker　　Day 19

Occasion	Mood	Food/Drink	Urgency Level
			Low Med. High
			Low Med. High
			Low Med. High
			Low Med. High
			Low Med. High
			Low Med. High
			Low Med. High
			Low Med. High
			Low Mcd. High
			Low Med. High
			Low Med. High
			Low Med. High
			Low Med. High
			Low Med. High
			Low Med. High
			Low Med. High
			Low Med. High
			Low Med. High
			Low Med. High
			Low Med. High
			Low Med. High
			Low Med. High
			Low Med. High

Quit Smoking Tracker   Date

Time	Number of cigarettes GOALS	Total cigarettes smoked
01:00		
02:00		
03:00		
04:00		
05:00		
06:00		
07:00		
08:00		
09:00		
10:00		
11:00		
12:00		
13:00		
14:00		
15:00		
16:00		
17:00		
18:00		
19:00		
20:00		
21:00		
22:00		
23:00		
24:00		

Quit Smoking Tracker   Day 20

Occasion	Mood	Food/Drink	Urgency Level
			Low Med. High
			Low Med. High
			Low Med. High
			Low Med. High
			Low Med. High
			Low Med. High
			Low Med. High
			Low Med. High
			Low Mcd. High
			Low Med. High
			Low Med. High
			Low Med. High
			Low Med. High
			Low Med. High
			Low Med. High
			Low Med. High
			Low Med. High
			Low Med. High
			Low Med. High
			Low Med. High
			Low Med. High
			Low Med. High
			Low Med. High
			Low Med. High

Quit Smoking Tracker   Date

Time	Number of cigarettes GOALS	Total cigarettes smoked
01:00		
02:00		
03:00		
04:00		
05:00		
06:00		
07:00		
08:00		
09:00		
10:00		
11:00		
12:00		
13:00		
14:00		
15:00		
16:00		
17:00		
18:00		
19:00		
20:00		
21:00		
22:00		
23:00		
24:00		

Quit Smoking Tracker   Day 21

Occasion	Mood	Food/Drink	Urgency Level
			Low Med. High
			Low Med. High
			Low Med. High
			Low Med. High
			Low Med. High
			Low Med. High
			Low Med. High
			Low Med. High
			Low Med. High
			Low Med. High
			Low Med. High
			Low Med. High
			Low Med. High
			Low Med. High
			Low Med. High
			Low Med. High
			Low Med. High
			Low Med. High
			Low Med. High
			Low Med. High
			Low Med. High
			Low Med. High
			Low Med. High
			Low Med. High

Quit Smoking Tracker

Quit Smoking Tracker

Quit Smoking Tracker   Date

Time	Number of cigarettes GOALS	Total cigarettes smoked
01:00		
02:00		
03:00		
04:00		
05:00		
06:00		
07:00		
08:00		
09:00		
10:00		
11:00		
12:00		
13:00		
14:00		
15:00		
16:00		
17:00		
18:00		
19:00		
20:00		
21:00		
22:00		
23:00		
24:00		

Quit Smoking Tracker — Day 22

Occasion	Mood	Food/Drink	Urgency Level
			Low Med. High
			Low Med. High
			Low Med. High
			Low Med. High
			Low Med. High
			Low Med. High
			Low Med. High
			Low Med. High
			Low Med. High
			Low Med. High
			Low Med. High
			Low Med. High
			Low Med. High
			Low Med. High
			Low Med. High
			Low Med. High
			Low Med. High
			Low Med. High
			Low Med. High
			Low Med. High
			Low Med. High
			Low Med. High

Quit Smoking Tracker   Date

Time	Number of cigarettes GOALS	Total cigarettes smoked
01:00		
02:00		
03:00		
04:00		
05:00		
06:00		
07:00		
08:00		
09:00		
10:00		
11:00		
12:00		
13:00		
14:00		
15:00		
16:00		
17:00		
18:00		
19:00		
20:00		
21:00		
22:00		
23:00		
24:00		

Quit Smoking Tracker   Day 23

Occasion	Mood	Food/Drink	Urgency Level
			Low Med. High
			Low Med. High
			Low Med. High
			Low Med. High
			Low Med. High
			Low Med. High
			Low Med. High
			Low Med. High
			Low Med. High
			Low Med. High
			Low Med. High
			Low Med. High
			Low Med. High
			Low Med. High
			Low Med. High
			Low Med. High
			Low Med. High
			Low Med. High
			Low Med. High
			Low Med. High
			Low Med. High
			Low Med. High

Quit Smoking Tracker   Date

Time	Number of cigarettes GOALS	Total cigarettes smoked
01:00		
02:00		
03:00		
04:00		
05:00		
06:00		
07:00		
08:00		
09:00		
10:00		
11:00		
12:00		
13:00		
14:00		
15:00		
16:00		
17:00		
18:00		
19:00		
20:00		
21:00		
22:00		
23:00		
24:00		

Quit Smoking Tracker   Day 24

Occasion	Mood	Food/Drink	Urgency Level
			Low Med. High
			Low Med. High
			Low Med. High
			Low Med. High
			Low Med. High
			Low Med. High
			Low Med. High
			Low Med. High
			Low Med. High
			Low Med. High
			Low Med. High
			Low Med. High
			Low Med. High
			Low Med. High
			Low Med. High
			Low Med. High
			Low Med. High
			Low Med. High
			Low Med. High
			Low Med. High
			Low Med. High
			Low Med. High
			Low Med. High

Quit Smoking Tracker   Date

Time	Number of cigarettes GOALS	Total cigarettes smoked
01:00		
02:00		
03:00		
04:00		
05:00		
06:00		
07:00		
08:00		
09:00		
10:00		
11:00		
12:00		
13:00		
14:00		
15:00		
16:00		
17:00		
18:00		
19:00		
20:00		
21:00		
22:00		
23:00		
24:00		

Quit Smoking Tracker   Day 25

Occasion	Mood	Food/Drink	Urgency Level
			Low Med. High
			Low Med. High
			Low Med. High
			Low Med. High
			Low Med. High
			Low Med. High
			Low Med. High
			Low Med. High
			Low Med. High
			Low Med. High
			Low Med. High
			Low Med. High
			Low Med. High
			Low Med. High
			Low Med. High
			Low Med. High
			Low Med. High
			Low Med. High
			Low Med. High
			Low Med. High
			Low Med. High
			Low Med. High

Quit Smoking Tracker   Date

Time	Number of cigarettes GOALS	Total cigarettes smoked
01:00		
02:00		
03:00		
04:00		
05:00		
06:00		
07:00		
08:00		
09:00		
10:00		
11:00		
12:00		
13:00		
14:00		
15:00		
16:00		
17:00		
18:00		
19:00		
20:00		
21:00		
22:00		
23:00		
24:00		

Quit Smoking Tracker   Day 26

Occasion	Mood	Food/Drink	Urgency Level
			Low Med. High
			Low Med. High
			Low Med. High
			Low Med. High
			Low Med. High
			Low Med. High
			Low Med. High
			Low Med. High
			Low Med. High
			Low Med. High
			Low Med. High
			Low Med. High
			Low Med. High
			Low Med. High
			Low Med. High
			Low Med. High
			Low Med. High
			Low Med. High
			Low Med. High
			Low Med. High
			Low Med. High
			Low Med. High

Quit Smoking Tracker   Date

Time	Number of cigarettes GOALS	Total cigarettes smoked
01:00		
02:00		
03:00		
04:00		
05:00		
06:00		
07:00		
08:00		
09:00		
10:00		
11:00		
12:00		
13:00		
14:00		
15:00		
16:00		
17:00		
18:00		
19:00		
20:00		
21:00		
22:00		
23:00		
24:00		

Quit Smoking Tracker — Day 27

Occasion	Mood	Food/Drink	Urgency Level
			Low Med. High
			Low Med. High
			Low Med. High
			Low Med. High
			Low Med. High
			Low Med. High
			Low Med. High
			Low Med. High
			Low Med. High
			Low Med. High
			Low Med. High
			Low Med. High
			Low Med. High
			Low Med. High
			Low Med. High
			Low Med. High
			Low Med. High
			Low Med. High
			Low Med. High
			Low Med. High
			Low Med. High
			Low Med. High
			Low Med. High
			Low Med. High

Quit Smoking Tracker   Date

Time	Number of cigarettes GOALS	Total cigarettes smoked
01:00		
02:00		
03:00		
04:00		
05:00		
06:00		
07:00		
08:00		
09:00		
10:00		
11:00		
12:00		
13:00		
14:00		
15:00		
16:00		
17:00		
18:00		
19:00		
20:00		
21:00		
22:00		
23:00		
24:00		

Quit Smoking Tracker   Day 28

Occasion	Mood	Food/Drink	Urgency Level
			Low Med. High
			Low Med. High
			Low Med. High
			Low Med. High
			Low Med. High
			Low Med. High
			Low Med. High
			Low Med. High
			Low Med. High
			Low Med. High
			Low Med. High
			Low Med. High
			Low Med. High
			Low Med. High
			Low Med. High
			Low Med. High
			Low Med. High
			Low Med. High
			Low Med. High
			Low Med. High
			Low Med. High
			Low Med. High
			Low Med. High
			Low Med. High

Quit Smoking Tracker

Quit Smoking Tracker

Quit Smoking Tracker   Date

Time	Number of cigarettes GOALS	Total cigarettes smoked
01:00		
02:00		
03:00		
04:00		
05:00		
06:00		
07:00		
08:00		
09:00		
10:00		
11:00		
12:00		
13:00		
14:00		
15:00		
16:00		
17:00		
18:00		
19:00		
20:00		
21:00		
22:00		
23:00		
24:00		

Quit Smoking Tracker   Day 29

Occasion	Mood	Food/Drink	Urgency Level
			Low Med. High
			Low Med. High
			Low Med. High
			Low Med. High
			Low Med. High
			Low Med. High
			Low Med. High
			Low Med. High
			Low Mcd. High
			Low Med. High
			Low Med. High
			Low Med. High
			Low Med. High
			Low Med. High
			Low Med. High
			Low Med. High
			Low Med. High
			Low Med. High
			Low Med. High
			Low Med. High
			Low Med. High
			Low Med. High
			Low Med. High
			Low Med. High

Quit Smoking Tracker   Date

Time	Number of cigarettes GOALS	Total cigarettes smoked
01:00		
02:00		
03:00		
04:00		
05:00		
06:00		
07:00		
08:00		
09:00		
10:00		
11:00		
12:00		
13:00		
14:00		
15:00		
16:00		
17:00		
18:00		
19:00		
20:00		
21:00		
22:00		
23:00		
24:00		

Quit Smoking Tracker   Day 30

Occasion	Mood	Food/Drink	Urgency Level
			Low Med. High
			Low Med. High
			Low Med. High
			Low Med. High
			Low Med. High
			Low Med. High
			Low Med. High
			Low Med. High
			Low Med. High
			Low Med. High
			Low Med. High
			Low Med. High
			Low Med. High
			Low Med. High
			Low Med. High
			Low Med. High
			Low Med. High
			Low Med. High
			Low Med. High
			Low Med. High
			Low Med. High
			Low Med. High
			Low Med. High

Quit Smoking Tracker   Date

Time	Number of cigarettes GOALS	Total cigarettes smoked
01:00		
02:00		
03:00		
04:00		
05:00		
06:00		
07:00		
08:00		
09:00		
10:00		
11:00		
12:00		
13:00		
14:00		
15:00		
16:00		
17:00		
18:00		
19:00		
20:00		
21:00		
22:00		
23:00		
24:00		

Quit Smoking Tracker   Day 31

Occasion	Mood	Food/Drink	Urgency Level
			Low Med. High
			Low Med. High
			Low Med. High
			Low Med. High
			Low Med. High
			Low Med. High
			Low Med. High
			Low Med. High
			Low Med. High
			Low Med. High
			Low Med. High
			Low Med. High
			Low Med. High
			Low Med. High
			Low Med. High
			Low Med. High
			Low Med. High
			Low Med. High
			Low Med. High
			Low Med. High
			Low Med. High
			Low Med. High
			Low Med. High

Quit Smoking Tracker   Date

Time	Number of cigarettes GOALS	Total cigarettes smoked
01:00		
02:00		
03:00		
04:00		
05:00		
06:00		
07:00		
08:00		
09:00		
10:00		
11:00		
12:00		
13:00		
14:00		
15:00		
16:00		
17:00		
18:00		
19:00		
20:00		
21:00		
22:00		
23:00		
24:00		

Quit Smoking Tracker   Day 32

Occasion	Mood	Food/Drink	Urgency Level
			Low Med. High
			Low Med. High
			Low Med. High
			Low Med. High
			Low Med. High
			Low Med. High
			Low Med. High
			Low Med. High
			Low Med. High
			Low Med. High
			Low Med. High
			Low Med. High
			Low Med. High
			Low Med. High
			Low Med. High
			Low Med. High
			Low Med. High
			Low Med. High
			Low Med. High
			Low Med. High
			Low Med. High
			Low Med. High
			Low Med. High
			Low Med. High

Quit Smoking Tracker   Date

Time	Number of cigarettes GOALS	Total cigarettes smoked
01:00		
02:00		
03:00		
04:00		
05:00		
06:00		
07:00		
08:00		
09:00		
10:00		
11:00		
12:00		
13:00		
14:00		
15:00		
16:00		
17:00		
18:00		
19:00		
20:00		
21:00		
22:00		
23:00		
24:00		

Quit Smoking Tracker   Day 33

Occasion	Mood	Food/Drink	Urgency Level
			Low Med. High
			Low Med. High
			Low Med. High
			Low Med. High
			Low Med. High
			Low Med. High
			Low Med. High
			Low Med. High
			Low Med. High
			Low Med. High
			Low Med. High
			Low Med. High
			Low Med. High
			Low Med. High
			Low Med. High
			Low Med. High
			Low Med. High
			Low Med. High
			Low Med. High
			Low Med. High
			Low Med. High
			Low Med. High
			Low Med. High
			Low Med. High

Quit Smoking Tracker   Date

Time	Number of cigarettes GOALS	Total cigarettes smoked
01:00		
02:00		
03:00		
04:00		
05:00		
06:00		
07:00		
08:00		
09:00		
10:00		
11:00		
12:00		
13:00		
14:00		
15:00		
16:00		
17:00		
18:00		
19:00		
20:00		
21:00		
22:00		
23:00		
24:00		

Quit Smoking Tracker   Day 34

Occasion	Mood	Food/Drink	Urgency Level
			Low Med. High
			Low Med. High
			Low Med. High
			Low Med. High
			Low Med. High
			Low Med. High
			Low Med. High
			Low Med. High
			Low Med. High
			Low Med. High
			Low Med. High
			Low Med. High
			Low Med. High
			Low Med. High
			Low Med. High
			Low Med. High
			Low Med. High
			Low Med. High
			Low Med. High
			Low Med. High
			Low Med. High
			Low Med. High
			Low Med. High

Quit Smoking Tracker   Date

Time	Number of cigarettes GOALS	Total cigarettes smoked
01:00		
02:00		
03:00		
04:00		
05:00		
06:00		
07:00		
08:00		
09:00		
10:00		
11:00		
12:00		
13:00		
14:00		
15:00		
16:00		
17:00		
18:00		
19:00		
20:00		
21:00		
22:00		
23:00		
24:00		

Quit Smoking Tracker   Day 35

Occasion	Mood	Food/Drink	Urgency Level
			Low Med. High
			Low Med. High
			Low Med. High
			Low Med. High
			Low Med. High
			Low Med. High
			Low Med. High
			Low Med. High
			Low Med. High
			Low Med. High
			Low Med. High
			Low Med. High
			Low Med. High
			Low Med. High
			Low Med. High
			Low Med. High
			Low Med. High
			Low Med. High
			Low Med. High
			Low Med. High
			Low Med. High
			Low Med. High
			Low Med. High

Quit Smoking Tracker

Quit Smoking Tracker

Quit Smoking Tracker — Date

Time	Number of cigarettes GOALS	Total cigarettes smoked
01:00		
02:00		
03:00		
04:00		
05:00		
06:00		
07:00		
08:00		
09:00		
10:00		
11:00		
12:00		
13:00		
14:00		
15:00		
16:00		
17:00		
18:00		
19:00		
20:00		
21:00		
22:00		
23:00		
24:00		

Quit Smoking Tracker   Day 36

Occasion	Mood	Food/Drink	Urgency Level
			Low Med. High
			Low Med. High
			Low Med. High
			Low Med. High
			Low Med. High
			Low Med. High
			Low Med. High
			Low Med. High
			Low Med. High
			Low Med. High
			Low Med. High
			Low Med. High
			Low Med. High
			Low Med. High
			Low Med. High
			Low Med. High
			Low Med. High
			Low Med. High
			Low Med. High
			Low Med. High
			Low Med. High
			Low Med. High
			Low Med. High

Quit Smoking Tracker   Date

Time	Number of cigarettes GOALS	Total cigarettes smoked
01:00		
02:00		
03:00		
04:00		
05:00		
06:00		
07:00		
08:00		
09:00		
10:00		
11:00		
12:00		
13:00		
14:00		
15:00		
16:00		
17:00		
18:00		
19:00		
20:00		
21:00		
22:00		
23:00		
24:00		

Quit Smoking Tracker   Day 37

Occasion	Mood	Food/Drink	Urgency Level
			Low Med. High
			Low Med. High
			Low Med. High
			Low Med. High
			Low Med. High
			Low Med. High
			Low Med. High
			Low Med. High
			Low Med. High
			Low Med. High
			Low Med. High
			Low Med. High
			Low Med. High
			Low Med. High
			Low Med. High
			Low Med. High
			Low Med. High
			Low Med. High
			Low Med. High
			Low Med. High
			Low Med. High
			Low Med. High
			Low Med. High

Quit Smoking Tracker   Date

Time	Number of cigarettes GOALS	Total cigarettes smoked
01:00		
02:00		
03:00		
04:00		
05:00		
06:00		
07:00		
08:00		
09:00		
10:00		
11:00		
12:00		
13:00		
14:00		
15:00		
16:00		
17:00		
18:00		
19:00		
20:00		
21:00		
22:00		
23:00		
24:00		

Quit Smoking Tracker   Day 38

Occasion	Mood	Food/Drink	Urgency Level
			Low Med. High
			Low Med. High
			Low Med. High
			Low Med. High
			Low Med. High
			Low Med. High
			Low Med. High
			Low Med. High
			Low Med. High
			Low Med. High
			Low Med. High
			Low Med. High
			Low Med. High
			Low Med. High
			Low Med. High
			Low Med. High
			Low Med. High
			Low Med. High
			Low Med. High
			Low Med. High
			Low Med. High
			Low Med. High
			Low Med. High

Quit Smoking Tracker   Date

Time	Number of cigarettes GOALS	Total cigarettes smoked
01:00		
02:00		
03:00		
04:00		
05:00		
06:00		
07:00		
08:00		
09:00		
10:00		
11:00		
12:00		
13:00		
14:00		
15:00		
16:00		
17:00		
18:00		
19:00		
20:00		
21:00		
22:00		
23:00		
24:00		

Quit Smoking Tracker   Day 39

Occasion	Mood	Food/Drink	Urgency Level
			Low Med. High
			Low Med. High
			Low Med. High
			Low Med. High
			Low Med. High
			Low Med. High
			Low Med. High
			Low Med. High
			Low Med. High
			Low Med. High
			Low Med. High
			Low Med. High
			Low Med. High
			Low Med. High
			Low Med. High
			Low Med. High
			Low Med. High
			Low Med. High
			Low Med. High
			Low Med. High
			Low Med. High

Quit Smoking Tracker   Date

Time	Number of cigarettes GOALS	Total cigarettes smoked
01:00		
02:00		
03:00		
04:00		
05:00		
06:00		
07:00		
08:00		
09:00		
10:00		
11:00		
12:00		
13:00		
14:00		
15:00		
16:00		
17:00		
18:00		
19:00		
20:00		
21:00		
22:00		
23:00		
24:00		

Quit Smoking Tracker   Day 40

Occasion	Mood	Food/Drink	Urgency Level
			Low Med. High
			Low Med. High
			Low Med. High
			Low Med. High
			Low Med. High
			Low Med. High
			Low Med. High
			Low Med. High
			Low Mcd. High
			Low Med. High
			Low Med. High
			Low Med. High
			Low Med. High
			Low Med. High
			Low Med. High
			Low Med. High
			Low Med. High
			Low Med. High
			Low Med. High
			Low Med. High
			Low Med. High
			Low Med. High
			Low Med. High
			Low Med. High

Quit Smoking Tracker   Date

Time	Number of cigarettes GOALS	Total cigarettes smoked
01:00		
02:00		
03:00		
04:00		
05:00		
06:00		
07:00		
08:00		
09:00		
10:00		
11:00		
12:00		
13:00		
14:00		
15:00		
16:00		
17:00		
18:00		
19:00		
20:00		
21:00		
22:00		
23:00		
24:00		

Quit Smoking Tracker   Day 41

Occasion	Mood	Food/Drink	Urgency Level
			Low Med. High
			Low Med. High
			Low Med. High
			Low Med. High
			Low Med. High
			Low Med. High
			Low Med. High
			Low Med. High
			Low Med. High
			Low Med. High
			Low Med. High
			Low Med. High
			Low Med. High
			Low Med. High
			Low Med. High
			Low Med. High
			Low Med. High
			Low Med. High
			Low Med. High
			Low Med. High
			Low Med. High
			Low Med. High
			Low Med. High

Quit Smoking Tracker   Date

Time	Number of cigarettes GOALS	Total cigarettes smoked
01:00		
02:00		
03:00		
04:00		
05:00		
06:00		
07:00		
08:00		
09:00		
10:00		
11:00		
12:00		
13:00		
14:00		
15:00		
16:00		
17:00		
18:00		
19:00		
20:00		
21:00		
22:00		
23:00		
24:00		

Quit Smoking Tracker   Day 42

Occasion	Mood	Food/Drink	Urgency Level
			Low Med. High
			Low Med. High
			Low Med. High
			Low Med. High
			Low Med. High
			Low Med. High
			Low Med. High
			Low Med. High
			Low Med. High
			Low Med. High
			Low Med. High
			Low Med. High
			Low Med. High
			Low Med. High
			Low Med. High
			Low Med. High
			Low Med. High
			Low Med. High
			Low Med. High
			Low Med. High
			Low Med. High
			Low Med. High
			Low Med. High

Quit Smoking Tracker

Quit Smoking Tracker

Quit Smoking Tracker   Date

Time	Number of cigarettes GOALS	Total cigarettes smoked
01:00		
02:00		
03:00		
04:00		
05:00		
06:00		
07:00		
08:00		
09:00		
10:00		
11:00		
12:00		
13:00		
14:00		
15:00		
16:00		
17:00		
18:00		
19:00		
20:00		
21:00		
22:00		
23:00		
24:00		

Quit Smoking Tracker   Day 43

Occasion	Mood	Food/Drink	Urgency Level
			Low Med. High
			Low Med. High
			Low Med. High
			Low Med. High
			Low Med. High
			Low Med. High
			Low Med. High
			Low Med. High
			Low Med. High
			Low Med. High
			Low Med. High
			Low Med. High
			Low Med. High
			Low Med. High
			Low Med. High
			Low Med. High
			Low Med. High
			Low Med. High
			Low Med. High
			Low Med. High
			Low Med. High
			Low Med. High
			Low Med. High

Quit Smoking Tracker   Date

Time	Number of cigarettes GOALS	Total cigarettes smoked
01:00		
02:00		
03:00		
04:00		
05:00		
06:00		
07:00		
08:00		
09:00		
10:00		
11:00		
12:00		
13:00		
14:00		
15:00		
16:00		
17:00		
18:00		
19:00		
20:00		
21:00		
22:00		
23:00		
24:00		

Quit Smoking Tracker   Day 44

Occasion	Mood	Food/Drink	Urgency Level
			Low Med. High
			Low Med. High
			Low Med. High
			Low Med. High
			Low Med. High
			Low Med. High
			Low Med. High
			Low Med. High
			Low Med. High
			Low Med. High
			Low Med. High
			Low Med. High
			Low Med. High
			Low Med. High
			Low Med. High
			Low Med. High
			Low Med. High
			Low Med. High
			Low Med. High
			Low Med. High
			Low Med. High
			Low Med. High
			Low Med. High

Quit Smoking Tracker   Date

Time	Number of cigarettes GOALS	Total cigarettes smoked
01:00		
02:00		
03:00		
04:00		
05:00		
06:00		
07:00		
08:00		
09:00		
10:00		
11:00		
12:00		
13:00		
14:00		
15:00		
16:00		
17:00		
18:00		
19:00		
20:00		
21:00		
22:00		
23:00		
24:00		

Quit Smoking Tracker   Day 45

Occasion	Mood	Food/Drink	Urgency Level
			Low Med. High
			Low Med. High
			Low Med. High
			Low Med. High
			Low Med. High
			Low Med. High
			Low Med. High
			Low Med. High
			Low Med. High
			Low Med. High
			Low Med. High
			Low Med. High
			Low Med. High
			Low Med. High
			Low Med. High
			Low Med. High
			Low Med. High
			Low Med. High
			Low Med. High
			Low Med. High
			Low Med. High
			Low Med. High
			Low Med. High

Quit Smoking Tracker   Date

Time	Number of cigarettes GOALS	Total cigarettes smoked
01:00		
02:00		
03:00		
04:00		
05:00		
06:00		
07:00		
08:00		
09:00		
10:00		
11:00		
12:00		
13:00		
14:00		
15:00		
16:00		
17:00		
18:00		
19:00		
20:00		
21:00		
22:00		
23:00		
24:00		

Quit Smoking Tracker   Day 46

Occasion	Mood	Food/Drink	Urgency Level
			Low Med. High
			Low Med. High
			Low Med. High
			Low Med. High
			Low Med. High
			Low Med. High
			Low Med. High
			Low Med. High
			Low Med. High
			Low Med. High
			Low Med. High
			Low Med. High
			Low Med. High
			Low Med. High
			Low Med. High
			Low Med. High
			Low Med. High
			Low Med. High
			Low Med. High
			Low Med. High
			Low Med. High
			Low Med. High
			Low Med. High

Quit Smoking Tracker   Date

Time	Number of cigarettes GOALS	Total cigarettes smoked
01:00		
02:00		
03:00		
04:00		
05:00		
06:00		
07:00		
08:00		
09:00		
10:00		
11:00		
12:00		
13:00		
14:00		
15:00		
16:00		
17:00		
18:00		
19:00		
20:00		
21:00		
22:00		
23:00		
24:00		

Quit Smoking Tracker   Day 47

Occasion	Mood	Food/Drink	Urgency Level
			Low Med. High
			Low Med. High
			Low Med. High
			Low Med. High
			Low Med. High
			Low Med. High
			Low Med. High
			Low Med. High
			Low Med. High
			Low Med. High
			Low Med. High
			Low Med. High
			Low Med. High
			Low Med. High
			Low Med. High
			Low Med. High
			Low Med. High
			Low Med. High
			Low Med. High
			Low Med. High
			Low Med. High
			Low Med. High
			Low Med. High

Quit Smoking Tracker   Date

Time	Number of cigarettes GOALS	Total cigarettes smoked
01:00		
02:00		
03:00		
04:00		
05:00		
06:00		
07:00		
08:00		
09:00		
10:00		
11:00		
12:00		
13:00		
14:00		
15:00		
16:00		
17:00		
18:00		
19:00		
20:00		
21:00		
22:00		
23:00		
24:00		

Quit Smoking Tracker   Day 48

Occasion	Mood	Food/Drink	Urgency Level
			Low Med. High
			Low Med. High
			Low Med. High
			Low Med. High
			Low Med. High
			Low Med. High
			Low Med. High
			Low Med. High
			Low Med. High
			Low Med. High
			Low Med. High
			Low Med. High
			Low Med. High
			Low Med. High
			Low Med. High
			Low Med. High
			Low Med. High
			Low Med. High
			Low Med. High
			Low Med. High
			Low Med. High
			Low Med. High
			Low Med. High

Quit Smoking Tracker   Date

Time	Number of cigarettes GOALS	Total cigarettes smoked
01:00		
02:00		
03:00		
04:00		
05:00		
06:00		
07:00		
08:00		
09:00		
10:00		
11:00		
12:00		
13:00		
14:00		
15:00		
16:00		
17:00		
18:00		
19:00		
20:00		
21:00		
22:00		
23:00		
24:00		

Quit Smoking Tracker   Day 49

Occasion	Mood	Food/Drink	Urgency Level
			Low Med. High
			Low Med. High
			Low Med. High
			Low Med. High
			Low Med. High
			Low Med. High
			Low Med. High
			Low Med. High
			Low Med. High
			Low Med. High
			Low Med. High
			Low Med. High
			Low Med. High
			Low Med. High
			Low Med. High
			Low Med. High
			Low Med. High
			Low Med. High
			Low Med. High
			Low Med. High
			Low Med. High
			Low Med. High
			Low Med. High

Quit Smoking Tracker   Date

Time	Number of cigarettes GOALS	Total cigarettes smoked
01:00		
02:00		
03:00		
04:00		
05:00		
06:00		
07:00		
08:00		
09:00		
10:00		
11:00		
12:00		
13:00		
14:00		
15:00		
16:00		
17:00		
18:00		
19:00		
20:00		
21:00		
22:00		
23:00		
24:00		

Quit Smoking Tracker   Day 50

Occasion	Mood	Food/Drink	Urgency Level
			Low Med. High
			Low Med. High
			Low Med. High
			Low Med. High
			Low Med. High
			Low Med. High
			Low Med. High
			Low Med. High
			Low Mcd. IIigh
			Low Med. High
			Low Med. High
			Low Med. High
			Low Med. High
			Low Med. High
			Low Med. High
			Low Med. High
			Low Med. High
			Low Med. High
			Low Med. High
			Low Med. High
			Low Med. High
			Low Med. High

Quit Smoking Tracker

Quit Smoking Tracker

Quit Smoking Tracker   Date

Time	Number of cigarettes GOALS	Total cigarettes smoked
01:00		
02:00		
03:00		
04:00		
05:00		
06:00		
07:00		
08:00		
09:00		
10:00		
11:00		
12:00		
13:00		
14:00		
15:00		
16:00		
17:00		
18:00		
19:00		
20:00		
21:00		
22:00		
23:00		
24:00		

Quit Smoking Tracker   Day 51

Occasion	Mood	Food/Drink	Urgency Level
			Low Med. High
			Low Med. High
			Low Med. High
			Low Med. High
			Low Med. High
			Low Med. High
			Low Med. High
			Low Med. High
			Low Med. High
			Low Med. High
			Low Med. High
			Low Med. High
			Low Med. High
			Low Med. High
			Low Med. High
			Low Med. High
			Low Med. High
			Low Med. High
			Low Med. High
			Low Med. High
			Low Med. High
			Low Med. High
			Low Med. High
			Low Med. High

Quit Smoking Tracker   Date

Time	Number of cigarettes GOALS	Total cigarettes smoked
01:00		
02:00		
03:00		
04:00		
05:00		
06:00		
07:00		
08:00		
09:00		
10:00		
11:00		
12:00		
13:00		
14:00		
15:00		
16:00		
17:00		
18:00		
19:00		
20:00		
21:00		
22:00		
23:00		
24:00		

Quit Smoking Tracker   Day 52

Occasion	Mood	Food/Drink	Urgency Level
			Low Med. High
			Low Med. High
			Low Med. High
			Low Med. High
			Low Med. High
			Low Med. High
			Low Med. High
			Low Med. High
			Low Med. High
			Low Med. High
			Low Med. High
			Low Med. High
			Low Med. High
			Low Med. High
			Low Med. High
			Low Med. High
			Low Med. High
			Low Med. High
			Low Med. High
			Low Med. High
			Low Med. High
			Low Med. High
			Low Med. High

Quit Smoking Tracker   Date

Time	Number of cigarettes GOALS	Total cigarettes smoked
01:00		
02:00		
03:00		
04:00		
05:00		
06:00		
07:00		
08:00		
09:00		
10:00		
11:00		
12:00		
13:00		
14:00		
15:00		
16:00		
17:00		
18:00		
19:00		
20:00		
21:00		
22:00		
23:00		
24:00		

Occasion	Mood	Food/Drink	Urgency Level
			Low Med. High
			Low Med. High
			Low Med. High
			Low Med. High
			Low Med. High
			Low Med. High
			Low Med. High
			Low Med. High
			Low Med. High
			Low Med. High
			Low Med. High
			Low Med. High
			Low Med. High
			Low Med. High
			Low Med. High
			Low Med. High
			Low Med. High
			Low Med. High
			Low Med. High
			Low Med. High
			Low Med. High
			Low Med. High
			Low Med. High

Quit Smoking Tracker   Date

Time	Number of cigarettes GOALS	Total cigarettes smoked
01:00		
02:00		
03:00		
04:00		
05:00		
06:00		
07:00		
08:00		
09:00		
10:00		
11:00		
12:00		
13:00		
14:00		
15:00		
16:00		
17:00		
18:00		
19:00		
20:00		
21:00		
22:00		
23:00		
24:00		

Quit Smoking Tracker   Day 54

Occasion	Mood	Food/Drink	Urgency Level
			Low Med. High
			Low Med. High
			Low Med. High
			Low Med. High
			Low Med. High
			Low Med. High
			Low Med. High
			Low Med. High
			Low Mcd. High
			Low Med. High
			Low Med. High
			Low Med. High
			Low Med. High
			Low Med. High
			Low Med. High
			Low Med. High
			Low Med. High
			Low Med. High
			Low Med. High
			Low Med. High
			Low Med. High
			Low Med. High
			Low Med. High

Quit Smoking Tracker   Date

Time	Number of cigarettes GOALS	Total cigarettes smoked
01:00		
02:00		
03:00		
04:00		
05:00		
06:00		
07:00		
08:00		
09:00		
10:00		
11:00		
12:00		
13:00		
14:00		
15:00		
16:00		
17:00		
18:00		
19:00		
20:00		
21:00		
22:00		
23:00		
24:00		

Quit Smoking Tracker　　Day 55

Occasion	Mood	Food/Drink	Urgency Level
			Low Med. High
			Low Med. High
			Low Med. High
			Low Med. High
			Low Med. High
			Low Med. High
			Low Med. High
			Low Med. High
			Low Mcd. High
			Low Med. High
			Low Med. High
			Low Med. High
			Low Med. High
			Low Med. High
			Low Med. High
			Low Med. High
			Low Med. High
			Low Med. High
			Low Med. High
			Low Med. High
			Low Med. High
			Low Med. High
			Low Med. High
			Low Med. High

Quit Smoking Tracker   Date

Time	Number of cigarettes GOALS	Total cigarettes smoked
01:00		
02:00		
03:00		
04:00		
05:00		
06:00		
07:00		
08:00		
09:00		
10:00		
11:00		
12:00		
13:00		
14:00		
15:00		
16:00		
17:00		
18:00		
19:00		
20:00		
21:00		
22:00		
23:00		
24:00		

Quit Smoking Tracker   Day 56

Occasion	Mood	Food/Drink	Urgency Level
			Low Med. High
			Low Med. High
			Low Med. High
			Low Med. High
			Low Med. High
			Low Med. High
			Low Med. High
			Low Med. High
			Low Med. High
			Low Med. High
			Low Med. High
			Low Med. High
			Low Med. High
			Low Med. High
			Low Med. High
			Low Med. High
			Low Med. High
			Low Med. High
			Low Med. High
			Low Med. High
			Low Med. High
			Low Med. High
			Low Med. High

Quit Smoking Tracker   Date

Time	Number of cigarettes GOALS	Total cigarettes smoked
01:00		
02:00		
03:00		
04:00		
05:00		
06:00		
07:00		
08:00		
09:00		
10:00		
11:00		
12:00		
13:00		
14:00		
15:00		
16:00		
17:00		
18:00		
19:00		
20:00		
21:00		
22:00		
23:00		
24:00		

Quit Smoking Tracker   Day 57

Occasion	Mood	Food/Drink	Urgency Level
			Low Med. High
			Low Med. High
			Low Med. High
			Low Med. High
			Low Med. High
			Low Med. High
			Low Med. High
			Low Med. High
			Low Med. High
			Low Med. High
			Low Med. High
			Low Med. High
			Low Med. High
			Low Med. High
			Low Med. High
			Low Med. High
			Low Med. High
			Low Med. High
			Low Med. High
			Low Med. High
			Low Med. High
			Low Med. High
			Low Med. High

Quit Smoking Tracker

Quit Smoking Tracker

Quit Smoking Tracker — Date

Time	Number of cigarettes GOALS	Total cigarettes smoked
01:00		
02:00		
03:00		
04:00		
05:00		
06:00		
07:00		
08:00		
09:00		
10:00		
11:00		
12:00		
13:00		
14:00		
15:00		
16:00		
17:00		
18:00		
19:00		
20:00		
21:00		
22:00		
23:00		
24:00		

Quit Smoking Tracker   Day 58

Occasion	Mood	Food/Drink	Urgency Level
			Low Med. High
			Low Med. High
			Low Med. High
			Low Med. High
			Low Med. High
			Low Med. High
			Low Med. High
			Low Med. High
			Low Med. High
			Low Med. High
			Low Med. High
			Low Med. High
			Low Med. High
			Low Med. High
			Low Med. High
			Low Med. High
			Low Med. High
			Low Med. High
			Low Med. High
			Low Med. High
			Low Med. High
			Low Med. High
			Low Med. High

Quit Smoking Tracker   Date

Time	Number of cigarettes GOALS	Total cigarettes smoked
01:00		
02:00		
03:00		
04:00		
05:00		
06:00		
07:00		
08:00		
09:00		
10:00		
11:00		
12:00		
13:00		
14:00		
15:00		
16:00		
17:00		
18:00		
19:00		
20:00		
21:00		
22:00		
23:00		
24:00		

Quit Smoking Tracker   Day 59

Occasion	Mood	Food/Drink	Urgency Level
			Low Med. High
			Low Med. High
			Low Med. High
			Low Med. High
			Low Med. High
			Low Med. High
			Low Med. High
			Low Med. High
			Low Med. High
			Low Med. High
			Low Med. High
			Low Med. High
			Low Med. High
			Low Med. High
			Low Med. High
			Low Med. High
			Low Med. High
			Low Med. High
			Low Med. High
			Low Med. High
			Low Med. High
			Low Med. High
			Low Med. High

Quit Smoking Tracker   Date

Time	Number of cigarettes GOALS	Total cigarettes smoked
01:00		
02:00		
03:00		
04:00		
05:00		
06:00		
07:00		
08:00		
09:00		
10:00		
11:00		
12:00		
13:00		
14:00		
15:00		
16:00		
17:00		
18:00		
19:00		
20:00		
21:00		
22:00		
23:00		
24:00		

Quit Smoking Tracker   Day 60

Occasion	Mood	Food/Drink	Urgency Level
			Low Med. High
			Low Med. High
			Low Med. High
			Low Med. High
			Low Med. High
			Low Med. High
			Low Med. High
			Low Med. High
			Low Med. High
			Low Med. High
			Low Med. High
			Low Med. High
			Low Med. High
			Low Med. High
			Low Med. High
			Low Med. High
			Low Med. High
			Low Med. High
			Low Med. High
			Low Med. High
			Low Med. High
			Low Med. High

Quit Smoking Tracker

Quit Smoking Tracker

Congratulations

You've come a long way – 60 days later,
I sincerely hope you've been able to break the habit
and are feeling the life changing improvements
 (and money savings) of being smoke free.

I am in control of
my life.